Tad

by Donna Duddleson
illustrated by Mike Reid

Practice Decodable 9

McGraw Hill Education

Bothell, WA • Chicago, IL • Columbus, OH • New York, NY

MHEonline.com

Send all inquiries to:
McGraw-Hill Education
8787 Orion Place
Columbus, OH 43240

ISBN: 978-0-02-146013-7
MHID: 0-02-146013-2

Printed in China

8 9 10 11 12 DSS 27 26 25 24 23

I am Tad.

There I am.

Am I sad?

Am I mad?

Am I Dad?

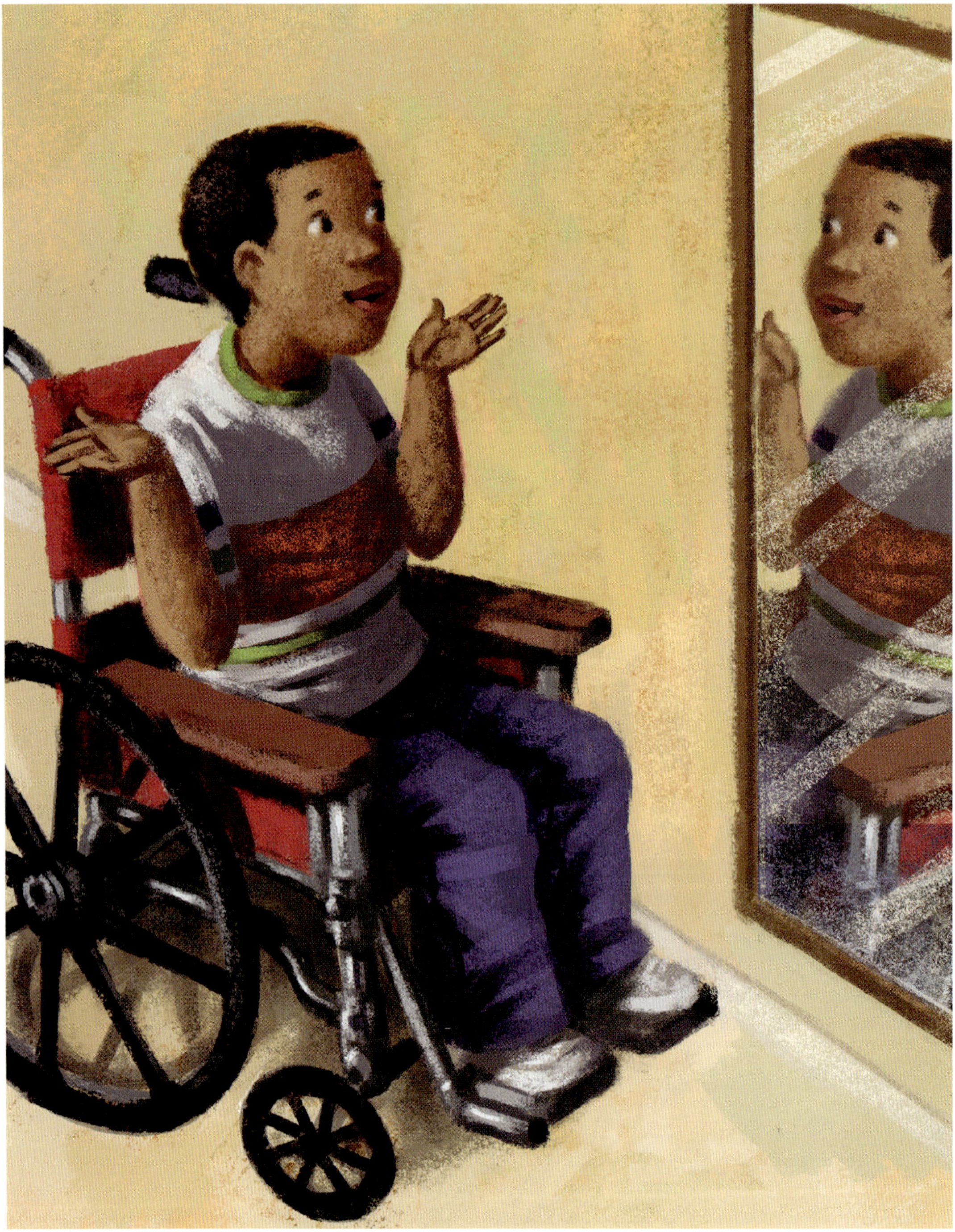

I am Tad!